St Ninian's Isle Treasure

David Clarke

Photography by Neil McLean

Published in 2008 by
NMS Enterprises Limited – Publishing
a division of NMS Enterprises Limited
National Museums Scotland
Chambers Street
Edinburgh EH1 1JF

Publication format, text and images
© The Trustees of the National Museums of Scotland 2008

ISBN: 978 1 905267 23 1

No part of this publication may be reproduced, stored in a retrieval system or transmitted in any form or by any means, electronic, mechanical, photocopying, recording or otherwise, without the prior written permission of the publisher.

The right of D. Clarke to be identified as the author of this book has been asserted by him in accordance with the Copyright, Designs and Patents Act 1988.

Publication layout and design by NMS Enterprises Limited – Publishing.

Printed and bound in the United Kingdom by Hugh K. Clarkson & Sons Limited, West Calder.

Map on page 7 by Marion O'Neil.

www.nms.ac.uk/books

Foreword

THE St Ninian's Treasure is both beautiful and mysterious; its craftsmanship is sophisticated, but its purpose, despite much investigation, is largely unknown. These exceptional silver objects, dating from about AD 800, include items apparently for secular and sacred use. The decoration reflects Pictish and Anglo-Saxon influences.

This publication provides a brief overview of the investigation into these objects since their chance discovery in 1958 under a cross-marked slab in the floor of St Ninian's church. This important treasure, found on the island bearing the name of the early Christian saint, became known as St Ninian's Treasure.

National Museums Scotland was delighted to work with the Shetland Amenities Trust to support the display of the Treasure in the new Shetland Museum on the occasion of the 50th anniversary of its discovery in 2008. This was one of the first results of a partnership agreed in 2008 and intended to lead to closer collaboration between the two organisations. The physical distance between Edinburgh and Shetland is very great, yet such partnerships help to close the gap.

Jane Carmichael
Director of Collections
NATIONAL MUSEUMS SCOTLAND
JULY 2008

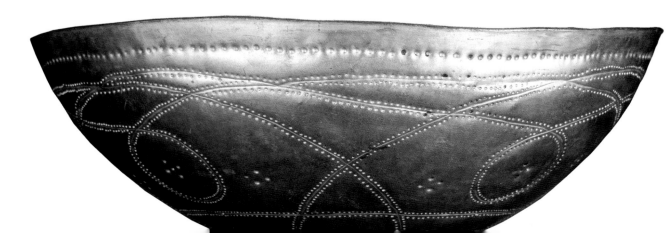

St Ninian's Isle Treasure

THE Treasure is a hoard of 28 silver objects. All are decorated. The main items are bowls, brooches and parts of weapons. It was found during excavations on St Ninian's Isle, Shetland. Most of the objects are considered to be Pictish. Consequently, they would have been made and used in the eastern and northern areas of Scotland. This is the largest surviving group of such metalwork.

The Discovery

The excavations on St Ninian's Isle were directed by Andrew C. O'Dell, Professor of Geography at the University of Aberdeen. There were five seasons of excavation from 1955 until 1959. The principal aim of the work was to locate and examine the medieval church that was known to exist on the island. It had been long abandoned, becoming ruinous and finally buried by sand. Local tradition identified the general position of the church, and the area was used as a burying ground by people living on the mainland. Burials had continued until the middle of the nineteenth century.

O'Dell's excavations established the precise location of the medieval church, but the remains were much disturbed by the later burials. Excavation in the immediate vicinity of the church revealed a group of burials in long cists – dug graves lined and roofed with stone slabs, and of sufficient size to enable the body to be fully extended. Such graves traditionally have been considered to be those of an early Christian community. But recent excavations have suggested that they might be the later part of a longer sequence of apparently Christian burials in this area, as below these graves were the remains of later prehistoric date.

The Treasure was discovered on 4 July 1958 by a schoolboy called Douglas Coutts, sent to dig in a heavily disturbed area in the nave of the medieval church. It was his first day. Turning over a

1. Opposite:
Silver bowl (detail of illustration 3).

broken stone slab with most of a cross incised upon it, he discovered the Treasure. It had been packed in a wooden box made of larch, a species of tree not then growing in Scotland. From the position of the objects, O'Dell believed that the box had been buried upside down, although there are no published plans or photographs that might help to confirm this. It is generally assumed that the Treasure was buried below the floor of an earlier chapel. This may well have been the case; the presence of parts of several early stone shrines certainly suggests a chapel in the vicinity. However, the excavation records are so poor that we cannot be sure.

Who owned the Treasure?

This is not an easy question to answer. When it was first discovered, strong attempts were made to suggest that most of the pieces were liturgical objects belonging to a local religious community. Fifteen years after its discovery, when the Treasure was published in detail, views had changed considerably. By then it was considered to be the treasured items from the household of a local Pictish lord. Without access to safe deposit boxes, burying your valued items in the ground at times of stress was probably the best option. Perhaps a church, if indeed the Treasure was buried in one, seemed a particularly safe place. Certainly, if O'Dell's view that the box containing the Treasure was buried upside down is correct, it suggests that the burial was done hastily under pressure.

But the absence of overtly religious objects in the Treasure need not mean that it belonged to a secular household. In communities without coinage these are just the sort of objects that represented intrinsic wealth independent of their intended function. The pieces are not all of the same date and the collection may have been put together over several generations. This scenario would as well fit the accumulating wealth of a religious community as that of an aristocratic family.

The Treasure

Apart from a fragment of the jaw bone of a porpoise, all of the objects are made of silver, although not always of very high quality. Some have parts that are gilded. The Treasure's contents fall into three groups: items connected with feasting, weapons, and jewellery. This grouping assumes that the enigmatic cone-shaped objects are decorative elements from a sword belt, scabbard or shield, although that may well not have been the case. All three groups are integral to expressions of aristocratic wealth and power in early historic Scotland.

Feasting

There are seven bowls and a more elaborate hanging bowl. The seven bowls cannot be regarded as a set although they may have been used as if they were. They show small but significant differences in size. And there is a similar range in both the manner of their decoration and in their decorative schemes. Four of the bowls have geometric decoration and in three instances this is combined with interlace. The motifs are created through the use of closely-set punched dots. One of these bowls has a central gilt mount inside it. The mount has complex cast interlace decoration around a central setting of red enamel. One of the other bowls has curvilinear designs that are dominated by that of a large equal-armed cross. The final two bowls have animal patterns. The animals have interlaced bodies and limbs. They are created by packing the background with punched dots so that the animals stand out as plain areas. These bowls are more likely to have been drinking bowls than used for food.

Hanging bowls are found throughout Britain, but most commonly in Anglo-Saxon England. The example in the Treasure is one of only three known bowls made of silver. It has three suspension rings set in the necks of gilded animals. Their flattened bodies are riveted to the walls of the bowl and their heads peer over the rim into it. There is a cast gilded roundel inside on the base of the bowl. This was matched on the outside by a silver roundel, now detached. The use of these bowls has been much debated. The most generally accepted view is that they were used as finger bowls during feasts, but suspended as ornamental features when not in use.

In addition to the bowls there are two other utensils in the Treasure. The spoon has a tiny dog's head at the junction between the handle and the bowl. The dog's eyes are made of blue glass and its tongue is extended as if licking the contents of the bowl. The other piece with a single curved prong is unlikely to have been used as a fork, an implement not seen in Scotland until many centuries later. It was perhaps used in eating shellfish.

Weapons

It seems likely that the parts that were found in the Treasure had been removed from their weapons before burial. They may all be from swords. Their presence, albeit from pieces more likely used for display than fighting, is important because we have so few surviving

2. Silver-gilt penannular brooch (width: 77 mm).

weapons from this period. The representations on Pictish stones show that swords were a clear symbol of rank.

The hilt is gilded. Its decoration consists of interlaced animals with dotted bodies. There are also two chapes with animal heads at each end. One of them is gilded. A chape is the metal fitting at the base of a scabbard that stops the sword point breaking through the bottom when the sword is inserted. One chape has two Latin inscriptions. On one side the inscription says INNOMINEDS, i.e. *in nomine d[ei] s[ummi]*, translating as 'in the name of God the highest'. On the other side the inscription reads as RESADFILISPUSSCIO. The interpretation of this is less straightforward but appears to be *res ad fili sp[irit]us s[an]c[t]io*, 'property of the son of the holy spirit'. In this view, this inscription forms the second half of the inscription begun on the other side.

The three cone-shaped objects are included in this section as decorative elements from a sword belt or scabbard, but this is by no means certain. They have each been attached to some other material through a pair of slots in their base plates. Although each has different decoration, they visually form a pair with a single, larger piece. The largest one is decorated with interlaced animals, while the pair have spiral designs and panels of animals and interlaced ribbons respectively.

Jewellery

There are twelve brooches in the Treasure. Many of them have areas of gilding. The pin of the largest brooch is now fragmentary but it may have been in good condition when buried. All of the other brooches are in good working order. The brooches are penannular with a break in the hoop through which the pin can pass. Apart from the largest brooch, the dimensions of the other eleven are remarkably similar. Yet the actual decoration and the form of the terminals vary from brooch to brooch. All of the brooches had settings, of coloured glass where they survive.

In early historic Scotland, brooches such as these did much more than act as cloak fasteners. The size and quality of the decoration signified the wearer's status and position in society. Access to such jewellery through the craftsmen who created them is likely to have been tightly controlled. In this context the presence of many brooches that are essentially the same size with comparable decorative schemes might strengthen the suggestion that the Treasure came from an aristocratic household.

When was the Treasure buried?

Without a clear understanding of the context of the Treasure it is difficult to determine when it was buried. Most have accepted O'Dell's claim that the Treasure was buried beneath the floor of an early church. A church, enjoying the protection of God, might well seem a particularly safe place to bury treasure in time of stress. This, combined with the conventional dating of the objects, suggested that the Treasure was buried at the end of the eighth or beginning of the ninth century AD. A convenient context was provided by the start of Viking raiding at this time.

But all of this is just interpretation based on what little we know of events in Scotland at that time. There is no clear supporting evidence. O'Dell never established the location of an earlier chapel so we do not know whether the Treasure was under its floor. Moreover, many of the objects show signs of significant use. None of the brooches retain all their glass settings, and in some instances they appear to have replacement pins. Yet it is generally accepted that they were manufactured in the second half of the eighth century. Is it likely that these valued pieces would have acquired such wear in less than 50 years? It seems more likely that we are dealing here with treasured heirlooms. In such circumstances the date of their burial may have been several centuries after the manufacture of the items. We know, for instance, that the Vikings were eager to acquire such pieces. All of this leaves open the question of whether the pieces were made in Shetland or arrived there some time after their manufacture.

∗ ∗ ∗

Further Reading

ALAN SMALL, CHARLES THOMAS and DAVID M. WILSON (1973): *St Ninian's Isle and its Treasure* (Oxford), Aberdeen University Studies, 152.

SUSAN YOUNGS (ed.) (1989): 'The Work of Angels', *Masterpieces of Celtic Metalwork, 6th-9th centuries AD* (London).

GEORGE and ISABEL HENDERSON (2004): *Art of the Picts: sculpture and metalwork in early medieval Scotland* (London), particularly pages 98-99 and 108-114.

This booklet was produced as part of a major research programme looking at early historic Scotland that is generously supported by The Glenmorangie Company.

The location of the find spot.

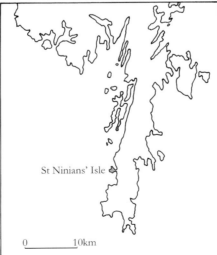
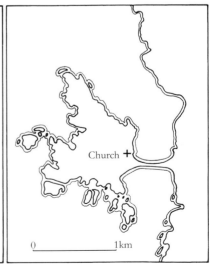

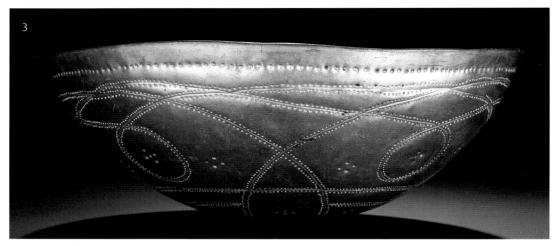

3. Silver bowl
(diameter: 151 mm)
with base of bowl detail (right).

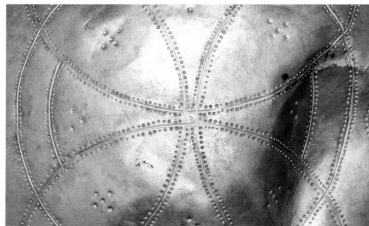

4. Silver bowl
(diameter: 145 mm).

4. Base of bowl detail from illustration 4.

5. Silver bowl (diameter: 145 mm) with base of bowl detail (right).

6. Silver bowl (diameter: 145 mm).

7. Silver bowl (diameter: 147 mm) with base of bowl detail (left).

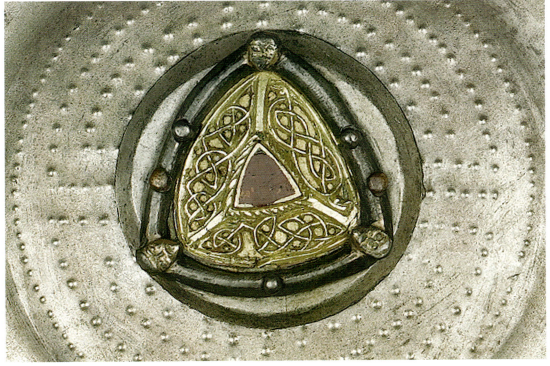

8. Silver bowl (diameter: 143 mm) and detail of gilt mount with red enamel inside bowl.

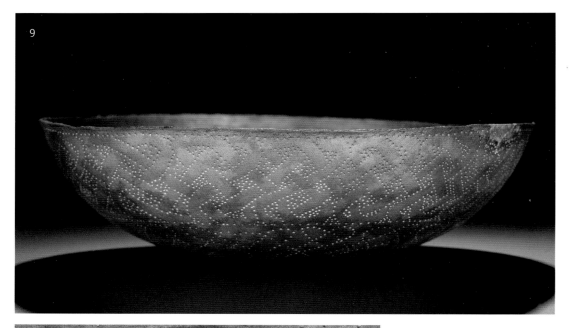
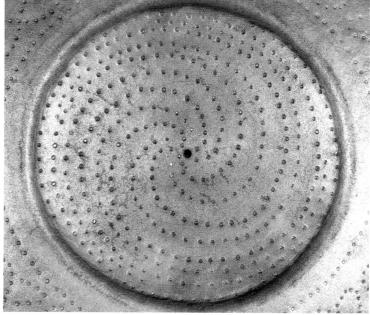

9. Silver bowl
(diameter: 130 mm)
with base of bowl detail (left).

detail (a)

detail (b)

10. Silver hanging bowl (diameter: 140 mm).

Detail (a) shows one of the three gilt mounts on the hanging bowl. They are in the form of spread-eagled boars. Detail (b) shows the underside of the hanging bowl with its central mount of silver foil. Detail (c) shows the gilt mount inside the hanging bowl.

detail (c)

11. Detail of dog's head on the spoon (left). The spoon is silver (length: 216 mm).

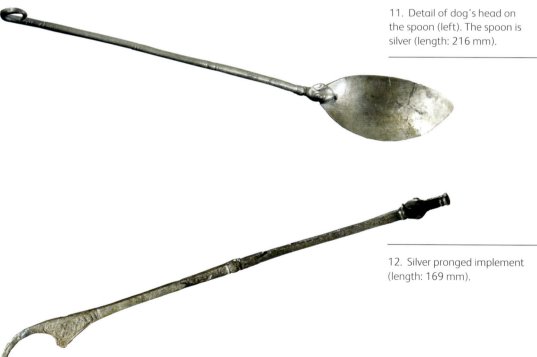

12. Silver pronged implement (length: 169 mm).

13. Silver-gilt cone-shaped object (height: 43 mm).

14. Silver-gilt cone-shaped object (height: 38 mm).

15. Silver-gilt cone-shaped object (height: 38 mm).

16. Silver-gilt pommel from the hilt of a sword (height: 55 mm).

17. Silver-gilt chape from a sword scabbard, inscribed on both sides (width: 81 mm).

18. Silver-gilt chape from a sword scabbard (width: 82 mm).

19. Silver-gilt penannular brooch; the badly damaged pin is not shown (width: 114 mm).

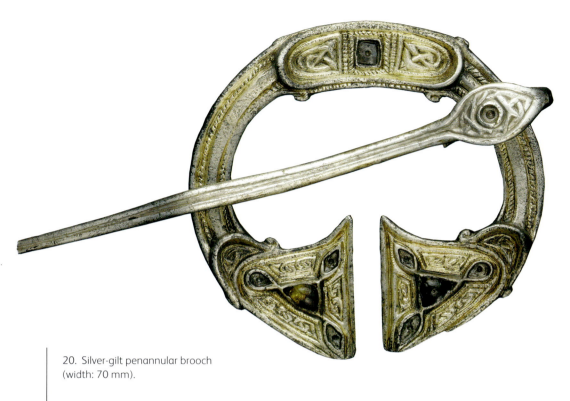

20. Silver-gilt penannular brooch (width: 70 mm).

21. Silver-gilt penannular brooch (width: 70 mm).

22. Silver-gilt penannular brooch (width: 74 mm).

23. Silver-gilt penannular brooch (width: 70 mm).

24. Silver-gilt penannular brooch (width: 65 mm).

25. Silver-gilt penannular brooch (width: 65 mm).

26. Silver-gilt penannular brooch (width: 70 mm).

27. Silver-gilt penannular brooch (width: 70 mm).

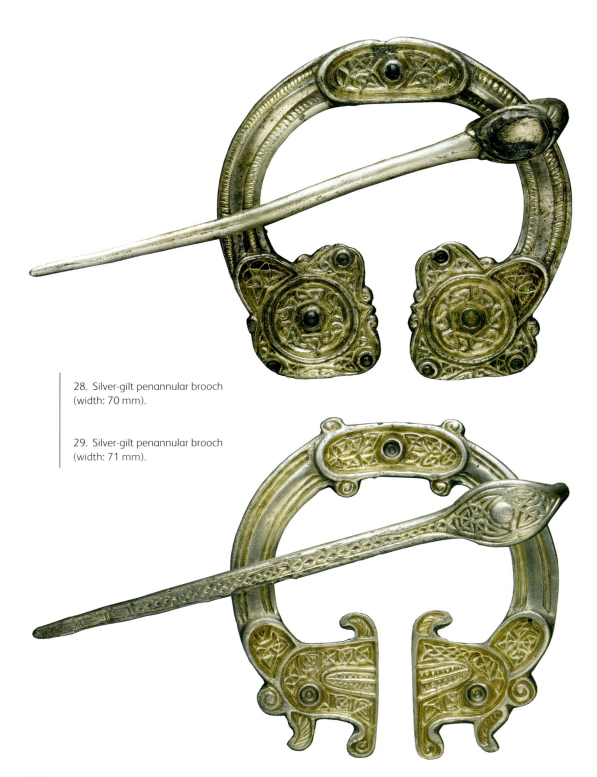

28. Silver-gilt penannular brooch (width: 70 mm).

29. Silver-gilt penannular brooch (width: 71 mm).